So, you're on a committee now ...

... a guide for anyone involved in the work of a committee

Michael Kindred and Malcolm Goldsmith

4M Publications

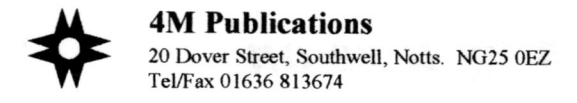

4M Publications
20 Dover Street, Southwell, Notts. NG25 0EZ
Tel/Fax 01636 813674

First published by 4M Publications 1999

Copyright © Michael Kindred and Malcolm Goldsmith

All rights reserved. No part of this publication may be reproduced, stored in a retrieval system or transmitted by any means, electronic, mechanical, photocopying or otherwise, without the prior permission of the publisher.

ISBN 0 9530494 3 4

Further copies may be obtained from 4M Publications at the address and telephone number given above. Discounts for quantity - please enquire

Printed by Roy Allen Print Ltd., Forest Road, New Ollerton, Newark, Notts. NG22 9PL

Contents

1	Coming to terms with Committees	4
2	What is the purpose of a Committee?	8
3	Are you in at the beginning or joining midstream?	9
4	Who are the actors in this Play?	13
5	The role of the Chairperson	18
6	The role of the Secretary	21
7	The role of the Treasurer	25
8	Drawing up an Agenda	28
9	Proposing a motion ..... and voting	34
10	Resignations	39
11	Writing Minutes	40
12	Confidential Minutes	50
13	Confidentiality	52
14	Standing Committees and Executive Committees	53
15	Sub-committees	55
16	The 'powers' behind the committee	57
17	People you might meet on your committee	61
18	A Committee is only a Committee	69
	Index	71

1   Coming to terms with Committees

The world is full of committees. Some of them are good, creative and important, and others - well, quite frankly they can be a complete waste of time. So how can you ensure that the committees that you are on are worthwhile so that you don't waste your time? Read on .....

There are many different sorts of committees, and there are many different reasons why they are set up. Some are there to manage or control something, and they are sometimes called *Management Committees*. Some may be formed to achieve a specific task: 'Let's form a committee to plan for the centenary'. Others may be there to monitor or evaluate something or someone: 'We've set up a small group to look into the needs of young people in our area.'

Whatever the purpose of a committee, its members are there to take responsibility. They are elected, nominated, appointed or invited onto the committee for a purpose, not to sit silently! If you are on a committee you are there because:

- You have certain skills, expertise or experience
- You represent a certain viewpoint or constituency
- You have ideas, contacts (or maybe reservations) which can be of use

... all of which other members of the committee need to be aware of.

Therefore: *be involved, be active!*

The Golden Rules for good committees are these:

- Prepare beforehand
- Be involved
- Explore the issues
- Make decisions
- Follow them up.

Committees tend to be bad, frustrating or ineffective when:

- They are unclear about their objectives
- People opt out, don't turn up regularly or don't contribute
- There is a lack of preparation before the meetings
- Decisions are sewn up by a small group before the meeting
- There is a lack of clarity about what has been decided
- There is a lack of follow up after the meetings.

When thinking about committees there are two lines of approach we need to be aware of - structure and process.

> *Structure* is about the shape, boundaries, responsibilities and technicalities of committees
>
> *Process* is about how they operate

In this booklet we shall be looking at how we can help to make them work more effectively.

A committee can have a good structure but if the way it works is not good then it will not be particularly effective.

Similarly a group of people can work really well together, but if the structure of the committee is not clear, then members may get very irritated and frustrated.

So, committees need *Good Structure and Good Process*

Committees are more accessible and welcoming when:

- they make sure members, including potential wheelchair users, have access

- everyone can hear properly. Has the chosen room got facilities for hearing loop systems or other aids?

- attention is paid to differing communication styles. Committees have tended to be made up of white, middle class people. Try to make yours as representative of its clientele as possible.

- people know where the nearest toilet is

- there are possibilities for a drink (water? coffee? tea?) before, during or after the meeting.

Finally, a word about how committees seem to have changed over recent years.

Many have become less formal, and in some ways a relaxed attitude can make for friendlier relationships and more enjoyable meetings.

However, a word of caution. A more informal approach can sometimes to go hand in hand with a laxness about things like timekeeping, confidentiality, thoughtfulness for the comfort of members, keeping accurate records, and so on.

So, informality should not be associated with slackness.

2 | What is the purpose of a Committee?

Are you clear about what the committee has been set up to do?

Confusion about its purpose will almost certainly lead to confusion about its decisions (or lack of them) and confusion about your role on the committee.

Some committees spend a good deal of time discussing things which are outside the remit or 'terms of reference' of the committee and over which members have no control. There is little point in spending a great deal of time discussing things that are not the business of the committee.

👍 So *be clear about its focus and about what it should or should not be discussing or deciding*

3   Are you in at the beginning or joining mid-stream?

If you are a member of a newly constituted committee, then everyone is starting more or less from the same place. 'More or less' because some people may have been giving more thought to the issues than others. But together, you are sharing in determining how the meetings will be run. You are starting with a blank sheet of paper, you are creating something from nothing.

If you are joining a committee that has already been in existence for some time, you will have both advantages and disadvantages, and it is important that you recognise these.

Disadvantages

- You may not know much of the past history of the committee and its meetings

- You may not know the names of the committee members

- You may not know people's particular hobby horses

- You may not be all that conversant with the subject or with some of the words used or people referred to

- You may feel more than a little intimidated and apprehensive.

So what can you do?

- Ask to look at copies of the Minutes (see later) of the last few meetings

- Talk to the Chairperson or Secretary (or both) and ask them to give you an overview of what is happening and of what the current issues are (or are likely to be)

- Do not be afraid to ask questions for clarification at your first meeting. You might well be helping someone else who also doesn't understand but who feels too embarrassed to ask! Cash in on the fact that everyone will be happy for a new member to ask questions (within reason!)

Advantages

- The fact that you are not part of the past history can be a very big plus - you are not identified with any previou disagreements on policy or between people

- You may be bringing a fresh outlook, a new experience or a dimension that is greatly needed

- You can ask the outrageous or awkward questions in all innocence, and in so doing you may be forcing other-members to review their position or to explain something that actually needs to be spelled out for other committee members.

So what can you do?

- You may feel able to plunge right in and make a major contribution to your first meeting

- On the other hand you may feel a little shy and unsure of yourself. Try to make sure that you say something at your first meeting, even if it is only to ask a simple question. This will help you to feel that you 'belong' and it will help the other members to get used to you.

Do you know how long you are joining for?

Good committees are usually clear about how long people serve on them; sometimes such things are spelled out in the Constitution. Beware of joining a committee without knowing what is involved.

Some committees have people on them who probably came over with William the Conqueror. This is usually bad news for the committee, for other members, for the person concerned - and possibly for you!

Committees tend to have their own 'style' and ways of working. If you are involved in a committee from the beginning you can help to shape and influence its style. If you join a committee which is already in existence you need to observe and reflect on its style. The way in which it operates will affect the ways in which you contribute.

Not all committees operate in the same way. You may be very happy and effective on one committee and feel unhappy and ineffective on another.

4 | Who are the Actors in this play?

The detailed roles of the 'actors' will be discussed later

a) Chairperson / Chair / Chairman / Chairwoman / Convenor

There is no title which now meets with universal approval. We use the word Chairperson throughout as this applies equally to men or women.

The Chairperson is usually appointed or elected by whoever set the committee up in the first place. Sometimes the members of the committee elect him or her themselves. The person may hold the position for a set number of years or indefinitely.

13

A few committees have a 'Rotating Chairperson'

This is a system in which different members of the committee assume the duties of the Chairperson for a number of meetings or for an agreed length of time. There are pluses and minuses to such a system.

Pluses

- Everyone gets a turn
- It is thought to be 'more democratic
- No-one gets landed with all the work!

Minuses

- Everyone gets a turn!
- Is the purpose of the committee to explore and experience democracy - or to get a job done?
- No-one does any work!

In our experience what works for the Council of Ministers in the European Community rarely works in Little Snodderington Tennis Club.

Some committees have a designated *Vice Chairperson* who stands in when the Chairperson is absent. Other committees ask one of the members to assume those duties as and when necessary.

b) The Secretary

The Secretary is the committee's scribe and (usually) its organiser. He or she arranges the meetings, informs committee members, takes notes, produces the Minutes and ensures that decisions are followed through and carried out. The Secretary is the committee's principal point of contact between meetings and handles any correspondence.

Some committees divide up the Secretary's work by appointing a *Minutes Secretary* whose specific job is to write the Minutes. Usually (but not always) a Minutes Secretary is not a full voting member of the committee, but is brought in to do that particular task. Occasionally one of the other committee members may assume the responsibility of being its Minutes Secretary, in which case, of course, they remain a full member of the committee.

c) The Treasurer

Not all committees have or need a Treasurer. If the purpose of the committee does not entail handling money, preparing budgets, paying expenses and the like, then there is no need to appoint a Treasurer. If there are *expense claims forms* to handle, to be passed on to a parent body to whom the committee is responsible, then the Secretary would be responsible for those.

d) Ordinary members

In addition to the above *Office Holders*, there are all the other members of the committee. It is important to remember that **all members of a committee are of equal importance.** Whilst, inevitably, some members are more involved, informed or committed to the work of the committee than others, and often people defer their opinions because of this, *everyone is on an equal footing.*

e) Co-opted members

Some committees, when they are created, are given the power to co-opt. This means that they may, as a committee, invite other people (who have not been elected or appointed) to join the committee. They may be asked to join for a specific length of time (eg: one meeting, six months, two years, indefinitely) or for as long as the committee is dealing with a particular issue. Sometimes co-opted members do not have voting rights.

Care needs to be taken to ensure that powers to co-opt are not abused. It is a facility to ensure that a committee has the necessary skills or expertise; it should not be used for by-passing the electoral system, as a reward for favours received or anticipated, or for packing a committee with people who have a known 'axe to grind'.

f) In attendance

Some committees invite people to attend their meetings (either on a regular basis or for a specific meeting). These are usually people who have a particular interest in the matters being discussed, or they may be employees or the chairperson of another committee. The extent to which they are involved in the meetings varies according to the particular style and ethos of the committee. People 'in attendance' do not have voting rights and do not carry the responsibilities of committee membership.

g) Observers

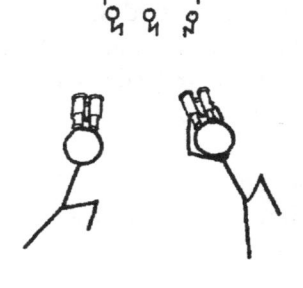

Some committees have people who attend as Observers. They are usually people who represent a particular interest or constituency. They do not have speaking rights (although they may ask if they can make a contribution - or may be invited to speak) and have no voting rights. They can be asked to leave the meeting at any time, especially when any confidential matters may be being discussed. In general terms, you only tend to get Observers at more formal types of committee and they are not a factor in the life of the vast majority of committees.

5 — The role of the Chairperson

First of all agree upon a name! As we have already said there is no title which now meets with universal approval. Throughout this book the word **Chairperson** is used as it is gender-neutral and does not imply or suggest either a woman or a man.

In most situations the Chairperson has the ultimate responsibility for the committee, in terms of ensuring that it does the work that it was set up to do.

The tone and ethos of the committee depend very much on the Chairperson and his or her importance is difficult to exaggerate. Having said all that, in some committees the Chairperson does very little more than preside at committee meetings and the actual responsibility for ensuring that the committee is a success is shouldered by someone else!

Handy tip! *It is a useful tip therefore, if you are on a committee, to work out who is actually taking responsibility (and where the power lies!).* The norm though, is that the Chairperson sets the tone and takes responsibility.

So what are the Chairperson's responsibilities and duties? Read on....

Before the meeting

- To be clear about the objectives of the committee, and to be fully conversant with its terms of reference

- To draw up the Agenda for the meeting (see later). This is usually done together with the Secretary. The Chairperson should be aware of the issues to be discussed, and of their relative importance, and of where decisions need to be taken.

At the meeting

- To welcome and introduce any new members

- At the appropriate time, sign the Minutes of the previous meeting

- Sadly, the Chairperson cannot automatically assume that all members have done their preparatory work/reading before the meeting begins, so he or she may have to introduce the items to be discussed and summarise the background to the discussion

- To control the meeting. Not in the sense of forcing through his or her own preconceived ideas (though this is a common criticism of many Chairpersons) but in ensuring that items are discussed fully and fairly

- To dissuade some people from talking too much and to encourage other people to talk a little more

- To ensure that everyone feels that they have had a chance to contribute and that their views have been heard

- To draw discussions to a conclusion and to summarise the arguments 'for and against' on any issue

- To be conscious of the time and aware of the time-needs of other items on the Agenda. Therefore it is important to start on time and for members to have some idea as to how long the meeting might last.

After the meeting

- To ensure that decisions are followed through. This is often done in conjunction with the Secretary

- The Chairperson is often called upon to represent the committee to other bodies, to be the spokesperson for the committee and to 'embody' the committee in between meetings.

Chairing a committee should be seen as a responsible job involving quite a lot of work and requiring considerable skill. It should not be seen as a reward or as a status symbol!

An uncommitted, unprepared or poor Chairperson can be the kiss of death to any committee, whilst a really good Chairperson can almost resurrect the dead - a skill sorely needed for some committees!

6 | The role of the Secretary

The Secretary is the Chairperson's right hand man or woman. **A good Secretary can make an enormous difference to the ways in which a committee works, a poor one can create confusion and uncertainty.**

The Secretary tends to be the administrator, the scribe, the prompter, the look-out person, the counsellor, the prop, the memory bank and the general factotum. If your committee has a good Secretary, cherish her, appreciate him, recognise that you have struck lucky! But what if you are asked to be Secretary? You will need pen and paper, time and a bottle of aspirins!

Before the meeting

- Ensure that the meeting room is booked, has enough chairs, is warm enough, etc. If refreshments are to be available (before, during or after the meeting) it will probably be the Secretary's job either to arrange them or to ensure that someone else is doing them

- Draw up the Agenda (see later) in consultation with the Chairperson

- Send the Agenda out to the members of the committee (giving them as much time as possible, so that they can think about the issues to be discussed).

At the meeting

- If possible bring spare copies of the Agenda and any other papers which have been sent out - there is invariably at least one person who has lost or forgotten theirs

- Bring any correspondence that has been sent to the committee since the last meeting, preferably having already discussed the content with the Chairperson before the meeting

- Take notes and write them up as the Minutes (see later). It is usual to check these out with the Chairperson before getting them photocopied and sent out to the members

- Make sure that all decisions taken are clearly noted, and make a note of which people are to do what jobs

- Have copies of the Minutes of the last few meetings (possibly going back a year or so), so that reference can be made to them if and when needed

- Have any other reference papers or literature which it might be helpful to have on hand

- Be ready to remind the Chairperson of anything he or she may have forgotten - in general terms, be there as their first helper

- Collect expense claim forms, if the committee has a system for reimbursing expenses.

After the meeting

- Tidy up the room etc (you may want to go there again!)

- Write up a draft copy of the Minutes and send/give to the Chairperson

- In the light of discussion with the Chairperson, write up the Minutes and send them out to all the members of the committee, and to any other people who might require copies

- Write any letters that might need to be sent, following the meeting

- You may need to remind people who have agreed to do tasks - perhaps a gentle reminder halfway between the last and the next meeting

- Act as the point of reference, point of contact for the committee between meetings. You may need to be in regular contact with the Chairperson, depending upon the nature of the committee and its business

- Ensure that you have full and accurate files. *It is especially important that you have a file of all the Minutes, duly agreed and signed.* All letters and their replies should be filed away. It may be a good idea to keep a note of telephone conversations, so that you can remind yourself of any dates or details agreed. The Secretary is regarded by the rest of the committee as being the person who has the facts and details!

Some committees appoint a ***Minutes Secretary*** whose job it is to take down the notes at the meeting and produce the Minutes for you to discuss with the Chairperson. Sometimes the Minutes Secretary is another member of the committee, and sometimes it is someone who is not on the committee but who comes in just to do that particular task. The Minutes Secretary is answerable to the Secretary because, however the Minutes are done, it is the Secretary's job to ensure that each meeting is accurately recorded.

Annual General Meetings

Some organisations are required to hold an Annual General Meeting (AGM) at which the audited (or otherwise externally verified) accounts are presented, and elections held. It is the Secretary's responsibility to liaise with the Chairperson about this. There are sometimes legal requirements to be met in terms of notifying people about the date of the AGM and relating to how people stand for election and how voting is to be carried out. Details of those requirements may be set out in the Constitution, or even by the Bank if accounts are involved.

The Treasurer needs to be reminded about the accounts well in advance, as quite a lot of work may be involved in preparing the accounts for presentation.

7   The role of the Treasurer

Not all committees have or need a Treasurer.

If a committee is handling money - receiving it from any source, and paying it out - then it needs a Treasurer. It is a great advantage if the Treasurer is financially competent! This doesn't mean that he or she has to be an accountant or a bank manager - but *this is not a job for the well-meaning person who just wants to help!*

Some Treasurers are so protective of a committee's funds that they regard it as tantamount to failure if they have to spend anything. To them, the success of a committee is directly related to its capacity to accumulate money. On the other hand, there are Treasurers who willingly spend money here, there and everywhere, and who are genuinely surprised when it is suggested that it would have been helpful if the committee had been made aware of its mounting overdraft. *Just because a committee is dealing with a worthy cause does not mean that stringent financial control is unnecessary.*

25

It is essential that accurate records are kept.
This is so important that it needs to be repeated!
It is essential that accurate records are kept.

So what are the tasks of the Treasurer?

- The committee may need to open a bank account. This involves completing a special mandate form, obtainable from the bank, before the meeting. The committee has to pass a special resolution - all the details are clearly set out on the form. You will need to decide how many people are authorised to sign cheques. It is strongly recommended that all cheques (certainly all over a certain amount) are signed by two people. *This is not a lack of confidence in the Treasurer, but a form of protection both for the committee and the Treasurer*

- It may be advantageous to open a deposit account as well as a current account, so that as much of the funds as possible earn interest. Your bank will advise on this and tell you how to transfer funds from one account to the other

- The Treasurer needs to keep accurate and detailed accounts - recording all monies paid in and all monies paid out. It is helpful if up-to-date information regarding the balance is available at each committee meeting

- To pay approved invoices

- To pay agreed expenses (it may be necessary to devise an appropriate expense claims form)

- To keep all receipts

- To prepare annual accounts and to liaise with an independent examiner of accounts

- To prepare a budget to bring before the committee (if appropriate)

- To give financial advice to the committee, so that it operates within its means

- To ensure that the committee has agreed appropriate procedures for the handling of financial matters - this will almost certainly be discussed with the Chairperson and Secretary beforehand so that an overall scheme can be put to the committee for approval. This may include discussions about travelling expenses and/or telephone calls made on behalf of the committee.

It is vitally important that no money is spent which has not been duly authorised by the committee. It may be that the Secretary needs a float in order to pay for photocopying and for stamps etc. This should be discussed and approved. Receipts should always be required.

A committee which has thought through its financial obligations and has agreed appropriate procedures can be a joy to work with. One which has not given thought to these matters will, in the end, not receive the support of busy people.

If a committee is employing staff, there are a whole range of fairly complex financial matters to deal with, beyond the scope of this booklet.

If your committee relates to a voluntary organisation, you can gain further help or information from your local Volunteer Bureau or Council for Voluntary Service (CVS) whose number will be in your local phone book.

8 | Drawing up an Agenda

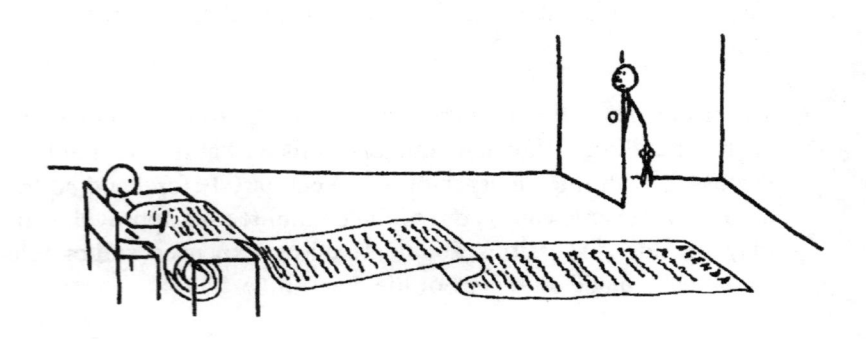

The Agenda for a Committee Meeting is usually drawn up by the Secretary after consultation with the Chairperson. It is sent out to all committee members before the meeting, giving them sufficient time to read through the papers and do any preparatory work that needs to be done. How soon before a meeting the Agenda is sent out really depends upon how frequently meetings take place. For a committee meeting once a month, probably a week before is acceptable. For a committee meeting less often perhaps two weeks notice should be given. For committees which meet very infrequently, it may be a good idea to send out a reminder perhaps a month before the meeting saying that the Agenda will be arriving in two weeks time.

It is a question of balancing the needs of committee members to have time to consider their papers, and the needs of the Secretary to give them up to date information.

What should be avoided, if at all possible, is giving people an Agenda when they arrive at the meeting.

What goes onto an Agenda?

- If at all possible, use a single sheet of A4 paper

- Begin at the top with the name of the Organisation, followed by the name of the committee. For example:

    Southwell Secondary School
    Parent-Teacher Association

- Then give details as to where and when the meeting is to take place For example:

    There will be a meeting of the Committee of the Parent-Teacher Association on (Day, Month, Year) at (Venue) at (Time)

- Then give details of what items are to appear on the Agenda. Almost all committees begin with:

    Apologies
    Minutes of the previous meeting
    Matters arising

- And many committees have one or two items which are always on each Agenda, such as:

    Correspondence
    Treasurer's Report

- And then include the items that you wish to be discussed. In general terms, deal with the most important ones first.

- **Matters arising** refer to things which were discussed at the previous meeting which may need to be talked about further, possibly to report on progress. It is helpful if these are listed on the Agenda, which means that they have been identified by the Chairperson and the Secretary in their earlier discussions.

If it is likely that one of the items will need quite a lot of discussion, then make it an Agenda item in its own right rather than a 'matter arising'. You may find it helpful to refer to the paragraph in the Minutes relating to the point to be discussed. For example:

> *Matters arising*
> a) *Letter to Chief Education Officer (3.1)*
> b) *Easter Holiday dates (5.3)*
> c) *Estimates for new cupboard (6.1)*

Handy tip! Some Committees spend as much time discussing the matter arising as they do the rest of the Agenda - there is always the danger that the previous meeting is re-run! Some committees therefore place 'Matters arising' near the end of the Agenda, and use it only for reporting on progress and action, and anything that needs greater discussion is made into an Agenda item.

- Some items for discussion may have papers which need to be referred to - these should be included with the Agenda when it is sent out.. The Agenda may say something like:

> *Discussion of new opening times (Paper enclosed)*

- If at all possible make it clear when the committee is just **discussing** an item, and when it needs to **make a decision** about something. For example:

    To hear about the recent trip to London
    Preliminary ideas for next year's Christmas Card
    To make a decision about contributing to the Sports Fund

- Most committees close with the item **Any Other Business (AOB)** sometimes called Any Other Concerned Business (AOCB). If at all possible, people should inform the Chairperson before the meeting that they wish to raise a matter here; if it is important or urgent, the Chairperson may then try to include it in the main Agenda business

    Handy tip! At the meeting, do not spend a long time discussing items brought up under AOB. If they are important, then they can be planned into the next meeting. If they are not important they should be dealt with quickly. Do not get into the habit of spending a lot of time on AOB - it can be very frustrating to committee members, and it can upset a carefully timed and planned meeting.

- Occasionally some committees try to put a time by each Agenda item, to indicate when that particular issue will be discussed and how much time has been put aside for it. This is not usual for most committees, but *(handy tip!) whoever is chairing the meeting should have a mental note as to how long each item should possibly take.* The overall length of the meeting is the Chairperson's responsibility, and meetings which go on too long will soon find that people vote with their feet!

- Try to make the Agenda look attractive! On the following page we set out a model Agenda as an example.

> **Handy tip:** Most committees seem to develop their own sense of time. Some need four hours for example, while others may be able to get through their work in 45 minutes. **Just because a meeting begins at 7.30pm, it doesn't have to take all evening** - its purpose is to get through some work, not to fill up an evening instead of going to the cinema!

If the Agenda is sent out a couple of weeks before the meeting, it is customary to send out the Minutes of the previous meeting with it. If the Agenda is sent out later than two weeks before, or if committee meetings are infrequent, then the Minutes are sent out by themselves, fairly soon after the meeting to which they refer.

Example

SOUTHWELL SECONDARY SCHOOL
PARENT-TEACHER ASSOCIATION

There will be a meeting of the Committee of the Parent-Teacher Association on Friday April 1st 2000 in the Dukes Committee Room at 7.30pm

AGENDA

1 Apologies

2 Minutes of the previous meeting (circulated earlier)

3 Correspondence
       Letter from Chief Constable
       Circular from Education Committee

4 Report on Fund-raising Social

5 The new 3rd Year Exams
       (paper from Head enclosed)

6 Treasurer's Report

7 Matters Arising
       a) Letter to Chief Education Officer (3.1)
       b) Easter Holiday dates (5.3)

8 AOB

9 Date of next meeting

9 | Proposing a motion ..... and voting

There are basically two types of committee: those which are conducted formally and those which are essentially informal.

That is both a helpful observation and an unhelpful one - it's a bit like saying there are two kinds of dogs, those which bite you and those which don't! On reflection, that is quite a useful thing to know when you are visiting someone!

Perhaps the majority of committees work along the lines of reaching a consensus, or a general sense of 'agreement' and decisions are taken which clearly reflect the mood and the will of the people present.

Other committees, particularly if they are dealing with financial matters or other matters of considerable importance, adopt a more formal approach to business, and this is clearly demonstrated by the ways in which decisions are taken.

In a more formal committee, before a decision is taken, a motion has to be *proposed*, that is, a particular person has to suggest that the matter to be decided is put before the committee. The person putting this *proposal* (or it may be called a resolution) is called the *proposer*, and before it can be voted on, some other member has to agree to support that proposer; this person is then known as the *seconder*. Their names would then be recorded in the Minutes.

So, for example, a committee may be discussing whether to spend money on a new computer. The Chairperson might say 'Have we a proposer for this then?' and Jim Sproggs (a committee member) might indicate that he is willing to be linked to the proposal; the chairperson will then say 'And do we have a seconder?' and Jenny Bloggs (another committee member) might nod or say that she is willing. The Minutes might then read:

> It was proposed by Jim Sproggs and seconded by Jenny Bloggs that a new computer should be bought. This was agreed by 7 votes to 2.

Occasionally, on some committees, some members might want the committee to discuss a certain issue, and they may do some preliminary work beforehand. They then send to the Secretary, in advance of the meeting, a resolution, which they have both signed, to be discussed at the meeting. For example:

> *It is proposed that the present computer be donated to the Sixth Form common room and that a new computer be bought, at a price not exceeding £1,500.*
>
> *Proposer: Jim Sproggs   Seconder: Jenny Bloggs*

Most committees do not operate in such a formal way, but even more informal ones may need to revert to this style when they are making controversial decisions. It is a form of safeguarding members, and means that if decisions of the committee are challenged at a later date, the background to the decision is clearly set out in the minutes.

> **Please note:** Different words are sometimes used which, in this context mean the same thing:
>
> Proposal = Resolution = Motion
>
> So a committee may discuss a particular proposal (or resolution or motion) - three ways of describing the same discussion!

If there is considerable disagreement whilst Agenda items are being discussed the good Chairperson allows these disagreements to be aired, but seeks to reach a consensus. This is not always possible and a vote may be taken to decide the issue. These discussions should remain confidential to the committee, so do not go round telling people who said what, and why! (see also Chapter 13).

Decisions are taken when a majority of committee members vote in favour (or against) a motion (or resolution or proposal).

This is usually by a simple majority, but in some cases under certain conditions, there may need to be (for instance) a two-thirds majority. This is often the case if the vote is about something to do with changing the Constitution, or making a significant change to the style or work of the committee.

For the vast majority of cases, committees operate in terms of simple majorities. Voting is usually done by raising your hand, and very occasionally there may be a call for a 'secret vote' (done by writing), but this is very rare. Some committees like to record the votes in the Minutes (passed by 7 votes to 2; or the motion was defeated by 11 votes to 8), others just record the fact that something was agreed, or passed.

Very occasionally you may read or hear the term *'nem con'*. It is short for the Latin phrase ' nemine contradicente' and means that a motion has been carried without opposition.

Sometimes, particularly on contentious issues, a committee member may ask for their name to be recorded against a vote. An example of this might be where, for instance, a church has decided to buy a new organ at vast expense, and one member bitterly opposes the decision - he or she may then ask that their opposition be recorded in the Minutes.

Once a decision has been reached, committee members are expected to accept and abide by it. Most people recognise that decisions are not always going to be to their liking, but that is the nature of democracy!

Some committees have one or two members who always seem to be 'agin the government'. They can be tiresome, *but they are needed.* A committee made up of 'yes men and women' or a committee which never generates heat or discussion is rarely an effective committee.

Handy tip! Try not to let disagreement over, say, item 2 on the Agenda affect your views on items 3 and 4, and remember that the arguments should be about the issues and not about the people!

The pluses ☺ and minuses ☹ of voting

The majority of committees probably get by without too much formal voting; the Chairperson guides the discussion until some form of common mind or consensus is reached. But care must be taken to ensure that this sense of trust is not abused.

Some people may feel quite angry or hurt if their opposition to (or support for) a particular issue is not noted. If someone is quite shy and does not participate in the discussions a great deal, they may feel that the absence of a vote totally ignores their contribution. On the other hand, too great a reliance upon voting can tend to split committees into various 'camps' or parties. This is where the skill of a Chairperson is needed!

Chairperson's votes

The Chairperson has one vote, like every other member of the committee. Some committees work in such a way that the chairperson doesn't use his/her vote very often, if the sense or mood of the meeting is clear. But if it is a case where there are strong views for and against a particular proposal, then the Chairperson casts their vote in the same way the everyone else does.

*If the votes for and against a proposal are equal, every member of the committee having cast their vote, then **the Chairperson's casting vote** comes into operation.*

In this situation, **and only in this situation**, the Chairperson has a second vote and the proposal or motion is passed or defeated depending upon the chairperson's casting vote.

10 Resignations

Occasionally (very rarely, in fact) a decision is taken by a committee which is strenuously opposed by one or more of the members. They may feel that it is fundamentally wrong, and they cannot accept or own it. They may wish their opposition to be minuted, and, in extreme cases, they may decide to resign from the committee. This is an ecceptable and honourable thing to do, and should not be the basis for 'bad blood' outside of the committee. People are allowed to have differences of opinion!

Resignation should be by letter to the secretary. Storming out of a meeting does not give a clear indication of a person's intentions!

11 Writing Minutes

It is the Secretary's responsibility to prepare and circulate the Minutes of the meetings of the committee. **Minutes are the official record of the meetings and they need to be filed away and kept.** They are extremely important and they must record any decisions taken. If ever there are disputes about decisions or about financial matters, people will always 'refer to the Minutes' and therefore it is important that they are accurate records. *What seems perfectly clear at the end of a meeting, may not seem quite so clear seven or eight months later!*

There are different ways of writing minutes and it is important that each committee is happy with the way in which they are presented. In the examples which follow, the same meeting is written up in different styles.

General rules

- Items should be numbered, and sections of each discussion should be sub-numbered; thus you may have an item which has three main points and they would be numbered in this way: 3.1; 3.2; and 3.3 (this is assuming that you are writing up item 3 on the Agenda)

- Make it clear when a decision has been taken and record **who** is to take **what** action

- Remember, these are the working notes of the committee. People may receive them a week or two after the meeting and they may be relying upon them to remind them what they have to do - so ensure that they make sense! They are also important records of the meeting for people who were not able to attend - so make sure that people who were not at the meeting can understand what went on.

Four examples of minutes of the same meeting now follow, with observations and comments on the way that they are written.

Example 1

**Minutes of the meeting of the Education Committee
held on December 17th**

1 Present: Miss M Smithers, Mrs D May, Mr J Jones, Mr J Long, Mr A White

2 Apologies: Mr C Quinn, Mrs B Young

3 Minutes: The Minutes of the previous meeting were agreed and signed. It was pointed out that Miss Smithers and Mrs May did not receive their copies of the Minutes until the day of the meeting

4 Finance: The Treasurer reported that there was £58 remaining the Current Account, but he was expecting a cheque for £12 later this month. After a lengthy discussion it was agreed to spend £25 on leaflets printed at Jo Bloggs publicising the winter course on Frugality

5 New Year School: A heated discussion took place on what should be the subject of the next New Year School. Miss Smithers thought it should be on Angels, Mr Jones argued for it to be on Inter-faith dialogue, but in the end Mr White's suggestion that it be on New Translations of the Bible was accepted. Mrs May thought it should concentrate on paperback versions. Mr Jones said that it might be possible to arrange a display.

6 Matters arising: Mr White reported that he had written to the Bishop. Mrs May asked whether the course on Frugality would be warm enough in the small hall.

7 AOB: Mr Jones asked whether other churches should be invited to attend these meetings and after a long discussion no decision was reached.

Observations

- They don't give the name of the parent body of the Committee - St John's Church

- They don't give the full date

- They don't tell us who chaired the meeting

- They are very descriptive - do we really want to know when people received the copies of the Minutes - *not unless a decision was taken* to ensure that they received them by a certain date

- Item 4 has more than one topic to report on, so it should have been broken down into 4.1 and 4.2

- Items 5, 6 and 7 have adopted a different format - the text is not indented - it is best to use the same format throughout

- Item 5 records things that were not decided - this is OK - some people like minutes to records other ideas (and who put them forward), other people prefer only decisions to be minuted. It is not clear whether any decision was taken as to whether it should concentrate upon paperbacks, nor is it clear what is going to happen about a display - is Mr Jones going to look into it?

- Item 5 gives a value judgement - a 'heated discussion' - whose judgement decided it was heated? Try to keep minutes neutral

- Item 6 - Matters arising: it is not clear what the letter to the Bishop refers to - there is no reference to any previous discussion. The question about the warmth of the hall does not appear to have been resolved

- AOB - this is clearly a major topic and should not really have been dealt with in AOB, but should have been placed on the APgenda of a later meeting. It is not clear what the next step is.

Example 2

St John's Church

Minutes of the meeting of the Education Committee held on December 17th 1999

1 **Present**
   Marion (in the Chair), Doris, Jim, John and Allan

2 **Apologies**
   Crispin and Barbara

3 **Minutes of the Previous Meeting**
   These were approved and signed

4 **Finance**
   4.1   Allan reported that there was £58 in the current account with £12 due.
   4.2   It was agreed to spend £25 on leaflets publicising the winter course - Allan would liaise with the printers

5 **New Year School**
   It was agreed that this should be on *New Translations of the Bible*. Jim would handle the preparations.

6 **Matters arising**
   3.1   John had written to the Bishop asking him to speak at the July meeting.
   4.   It was agreed that the course on Frugality should take place in the Meeting Room

7 **AOB**   The question of inviting other churches to attend the Education Committee was referred to the next meeting

Observations

- Note that first names are used. This is acceptable for a small, relatively informal committee.

- Items 4.2 and 5 record both the decisions and who is taking responsibility to execute them

- Typing the title of the New Year School (item 5) in italics makes it easier to read and remember

- Matters arising 3.1 indicates which section of the previous minutes is being referred to and reminds people what it was about

- The vexed question lobbed-in under AOB was (quite rightly) referred to a future meeting

- Note how the text relating to the AOB heading starts at the side of it, whereas the text relating to each of the other headings starts underneath. It's a small point, but it enhances the presentation to keep the same format throughout.

Example 3

St John's Church

Minutes of the Education Committee
held on December 17th 1999

1. **Present**
   Marion (in the Chair); Doris, Jim, John and Allan

2. **Apologies**
   Crispin and Barbara

3. **Minutes**
   Agreed and signed

4. **Finance**
   4.1 Allan reported that there was £58 in the current a/c, with £12 due.
   4.2 <u>It was agreed</u> to spend £25 on leaflets publicising the winter course - (**ACTION** - ALLAN - liaise with printers)

5. **New Year School**
   <u>It was Agreed</u> that this should be on *New Translations of the Bible*. (**ACTION** - JIM to handle the preparations)

6. **Matters arising**
   3.1 John had written to the Bp re speaking at July Mtg
   4.   <u>It was Agreed</u> that the course on Frugality should take place in the Mtg Room

7. **AOB**
   <u>It was Agreed</u> that the next Mtg should consider the question of inviting other churches to attend these committee mtgs

46

Observations

- The headings again clearly locate the meeting and its date

- The style is now getting very terse - some people may think too much so

- Agreements and Responsibilities for action are clearly indicated

- Some people do not like the use of <u>underlining</u>, and prefer **bold** or *italics*.

Example 4

St John's Church

Minutes of the Education Committee held on December 17th 1999   *Action/date*

1. **Present**
   Marion (in the Chair); Doris, Jim, John and Allan

2. **Apologies**
   Crispin and Barbara

3. **Minutes**
   Agreed and signed

4. **Finance**
   4.1 Allan reported that there was £58 in the current a/c, with £12 due.
   4.2 <u>It was agreed</u> to spend £25 on leaflets publicising the winter course   *ALLAN - liaise with printers: 18.01.00*

5. **New Year School**
   <u>It was Agreed</u> that this should be on *New Translations of the Bible*.   *JIM to handle preparations: next meeting*

6. **Matters arising**
   3.1 John had written to the Bp re speaking at July Mtg
   4. <u>It was Agreed</u> that the course on Frugality should take place in the Mtg Room

7. **AOB**
   <u>It was Agreed</u> that the next Mtg should consider the question of inviting other churches to attend these committee mtgs

Date of next meeting: 11.02.00 at 8.00pm

Observations

- The *Action column* clearly sets out what needs to be done, by whom, and when

- The date of the next meeting is confirmed at the bottom of the Minutes, which is a help to anyone who isn't sure if they noted it correctly when it was fixed at the meeting.

General comments

What becomes clear is that there is *no one right way* to write Minutes. Each committee will develop its own style, but what is important is that the Minutes are informative and that they:

👍 **Indicate decisions taken,** and

👍 **Locate responsibility for actions**

It is normal practice for the Secretary to send a draft copy of the Minutes to the Chairperson so that any corrections or alterations can be made before they are circulated.

> **NB: Minutes should be a record of what took place, NOT what you would have liked to have taken place!!!**

12 Confidential Minutes

Sometimes discussions take place which are confidential, and occasionally the Chairperson may ask the Secretary not to minute a particular discussion. However, **whenever decisions are taken** by the committee these must be minuted.

If a decision is of a confidential nature there are two ways in which this may be handled:

1   Some Committees also keep a *Confidential Minute Book*. This is a record of decisions taken but it is not open to public scrutiny. It is particularly appropriate when there are matters of a disciplinary nature to be recorded, or it may list salary levels. In these circumstances the official Minutes may say something like this:

    'Salary levels for the following year were discussed and agreed and these are set out in full in the Confidential Minute Book.'

2	Decisions reached may be added as a footnote to the Minutes which are circulated to committee members, but are **not** added to those copies of the Minutes which receive a wider circulation - such as to Observers, the Press or the Parent Body, etc. This is clearly not such a tightly controlled system as having a Confidential Minute Book.

13 Confidentiality

Regard the meetings of committees as being confidential, even if that hasn't been stressed. People must be able to express their views without fearing that everyone will know what they think.

On no account speak to the press (or radio) about a decision reached or the dealings of the committee, unless you have been authorised to do so by the committee.

Some committees have to work on confidential matters, and their discussion and papers must remain confidential. Other committees are more relaxed and open and they are not dealing with sensitive issues.

14 Standing Committees and Executive Committees

Standing Committee   **Executive Committee**

Some organisations are governed by a very large elected body which may meet only once or twice a year - a national church, for instance. It is usual for such bodies to have a *Standing Committee* to carry forward its business between the large, infrequent assemblies, synods or conferences (depending upon the name used).

Most of the information contained in this booklet is applicable to Standing Committees, but if you find yourself elected onto one of those, it is highly likely that you have already mastered everything contained in these pages!

If a Committee is very large (and it may be large because it is composed of people who are representing other bodies or particular interest groups) then it is often impossible to get through the business effectively, especially if decisions have to be taken which are complex or which need to be taken quickly.

Those sorts of committees often elect an **Executive Committee** to do the day to day work and to make decisions on behalf of the full committee. In these situations, the general committee tends merely to 'rubber-stamp' the decisions of the Executive Committee.

However, it is important that the Executive Committee communicates well and does not take its position for granted, because every now and then there can be a revolt from the ranks. *It always has to be remembered that ultimate power rests with the ordinary committee and not with the Executive Committee*, which can be dismantled or changed if the larger committee so wishes!

Handy tip: There is a close relationship between good communication and trust

15 Sub-committees

Some sub-committees can be unworkable!

If a committee has a lot of work to do, it may divide that work up by creating sub-committees. A sub-committee works very much like other committees, but it is answerable to the parent body (the main committee, and it only exists to do the work passed on to it by the main committee). Sometimes a committee has almost permanent sub-committees, whilst at other times it may create a sub-committee for a finite period of time, to do a specific piece of work.

Like any other committee, a sub-committee needs a Chairperson and it needs someone to take notes and act as Secretary - so that the deliberations of the sub-committee can be reported back to the main committee. It will need an Agenda, and it will need minutes, and it operates as any other committee.

A sub-committee is quite often chaired by someone who is a member of the main (or parent) committee; and it may have several members who are also members of the main committee, but it may also (but not always, and not necessarily) have some members who are brought onto it for their particular skills and expertise.

A great many organisations will have, for instance, a Finance Sub-Committee, which deals with the nitty-gritty financial matters and thus relieves the main committee of a great deal of work. The deliberations, decisions or advice of the sub-committees are then brought to the agenda of the main committee.

Sometimes sub-committees are asked to do some preliminary thinking and advise the main committee, and sometimes they are given executive authority (within agreed limits) to act on behalf of the main committee - for instance, a Parent-Teacher Committee may ask a sub-committee to organise a dance, and free a certain amount of money in advance to be used for publicity and other arrangements. In such a situation, the sub-committee gets on with its work and organises the dance, and the matter will appear on the Agenda of the main committee in the form of a report.

In some organisations there are **Pendant Committees.** These are similar to sub-committees, but may have rather more authority. They are called *pendant* because they 'hang' from the parent committee.

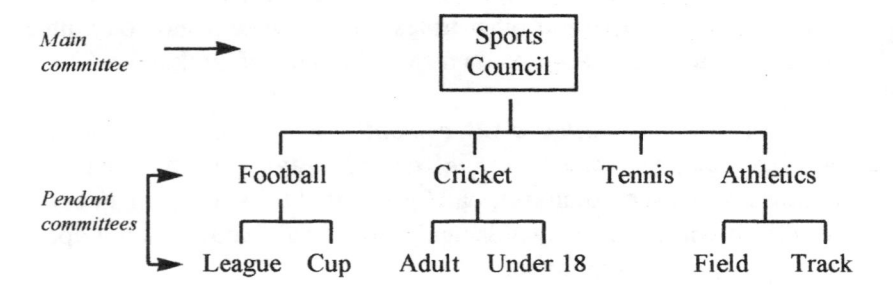

```
Main committee  →         Sports Council
                    ┌────────┬────────┬────────┐
Pendant          Football  Cricket  Tennis  Athletics
committees       ┌──┴──┐   ┌──┴──┐          ┌──┴──┐
              League Cup  Adult Under 18   Field Track
```

16   The 'powers' behind the committee

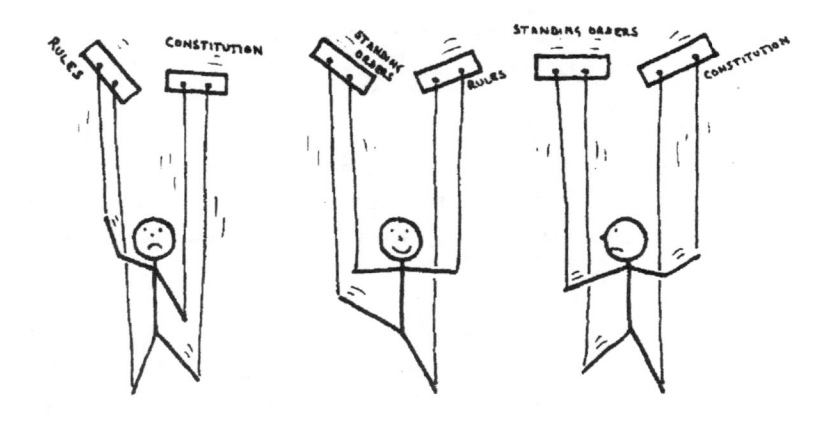

It is important that Committees are not dominated or manipulated by just one or two people, so there are usually rules determining how they should be set up and how they should be run. These are usually contained in the *Constitution*.

The *Constitution* is the binding document behind most committees. It usually sets out, for example:

- how many people should serve on the committee

- what officers there should be (such as Chairperson, Vice Chairperson, Secretary, etc)

- how long these officers should serve

- how many meetings there should be (monthly or quarterly, etc)

- what constitutes a *Quorum*.

There may also be *Standing Orders* which are a guide as to how business is to be handled and what may or may not be done.

Anyone joining a committee for the first time should get to know the 'powers' behind the committee. They are there to safeguard the work of the committee - and ultimately to safeguard the members of the committee.

Most people, on most committees, will not have to bother about such details, but if you are going to become a 'committee person' and serve on lots of different committees, then you will need to be able to find your way round such issues as Constitutions and Standing Orders.

Like many things which are a blessing - these helpful 'powers' can also sometimes be a real irritation, especially if your committee includes one or two people who fancy themselves as 'experts' and who keep referring to the Constitution or the Standing Orders. At times like this, these 'powers' can be a real brake on progress, but they are there for a purpose, and that purpose is the ultimate good of the committee and to enable it to get on with the work that it exists to promote.

Apart from setting out the structure of the committee - how many people are on it, how long they serve for, how they are appointed or elected and so forth, these background 'powers' also state what constitutes a *Quorum*.

A Quorum is the number of voting members of a committee who have to be at a meeting in order for the decisions of that meeting to be legally binding.

It is a very important safeguard, so that a few unscrupulous members cannot manipulate or hi-jack a committee and make decisions in people's absence which they know a full committee would not approve of. That is putting it at its baldest, but most committees are fortunately not made up of unscrupulous people.

It is, however, important that decisions are made which represent the weight of opinion of the committee and which are not the hobby-horse of one or two particular members. Usually, a quorum is about 55 or 60% of the members, so a committee of 12 may have a quorum of 7 - which means that if there are 6 or less people attending, then any decisions taken can only be provisional, and they must be endorsed by the committee at the next meeting.

A meeting is said to be *inquorate* if it doesn't have enough people to authorise its decisions.

Of course, most committees just get on with their business, welcoming as many members as can get to the meetings. However, if a committee regularly fails to attract a quorum, then *this is usually a sign that there is something radically wrong with the committee,* and questions need to be asked, such as

- Is it expecting too many people to be present - should the number be lower? In which case the Constitution may have to be changed.

- Are people staying away because the meetings are unsatisfactory? What might be the reasons for that? Wrong time? Poor management of the material? People not committed to the subject?

Handy tip! As a rule of thumb, committees should expect to have an attendance of 80% of members at most meetings, and if it is an important committee, dealing with important issues, then that figure should be much higher. Some committees expect 100% attendance, and it is not unreasonable to make that the norm!

Committees can be rendered ineffective and be thought to be a waste of time by some people if there is not a commitment on the part of all members to attend the meetings.

Some committees, at the end of each year, publish the attendance record of the different committee members. This can be a helpful procedure if members are elected from a large body, because it means that the people who voted for them can see how seriously they have taken the responsibilities of membership. Attendance is not the only way of showing commitment, and some people may attend all meetings and make little contribution, whilst others may miss some meetings but do a lot of work before and after the meetings - but attendance is one way of making a judgement.

If you cannot attend a meeting you should always send your apologies, preferably in writing, to the Secretary before the meeting.

ATTENDANCE RECORD FOR 12 MEETINGS IN 1999	
B. NEWSENSE	0
Y. BOTHA	0
IVAN X KUSE	0
B.O. WRECKS	12
PETER DOWT	0
SIR TINLEY KNOTT	0
MR. MAWL	0
U. R. JOE KING	0
C. U. SOONE	0

17 | People you might meet on your committee

There's a saying in Yorkshire: 'There's nowt so queer as folk' and certainly your experiences on committees will bear this out!

Because people are different, with different backgrounds, different views, different hopes and different fears - no two committees are the same. **You will bring to any committee that you are on, specific gifts and insights - but you will also need the gifts and insights that other people may have to offer.** Committees work best when the contributions that different people have to offer are recognised and valued.

What follows now is a caricature of different types of people. It is part fun, but it is also very much part truth, and your work on the committee could be helped considerably if you were able to recognise some of these different types of people and learn how to work with them - you might also identify yourself in the process!

The extrovert

- Extroverts are people who think with their mouths! They tend to talk quite a lot and usually have something to say about most things on the Agenda. What you need to understand is that their *talking is their way of coming to grips with the issue.* They are thinking things through as they speak, and they are quite happy to be challenged (usually!), and to be given a different point of view

- They express their emotions openly - so you know when they are annoyed or angry! Don't allow yourself to be bullied by them

- Sometimes it is necessary to discover ways of shutting these people up! They have a view on everything, whether that view is relevant or not! They often enjoy committees, but may not always do much thinking work before the meeting, and therefore they often 'fly by the seat of their pants'.

The introvert

- Introverts tend to be much quieter and sometimes it is quite hard work getting them to express an opinion.

They may sit on a committee and hardly ever say a word unless they are encouraged to speak. If the extrovert does his thinking whilst he or she talks, the introvert may do a lot of thinking and never talk! A good Chairperson will make sure that these people are not pushed out of the discussion by extroverts

- They are often difficult to 'read' in the sense that their facial expression or body language may not reveal what they are really thinking

- Very often introverts have studied the Agenda in detail before the meeting and they have reached fairly clear ideas about where they stand on particular issues. They may be quite difficult to budge on an issue once they have decided about it.

The visionary

- This is the person who loves dreaming dreams and is never more happy than when discussing some possible future plan in the broadest of detail. They tend to enjoy complex issues and love the opportunity to solve problems

- They are often bored by details, and if you rely on them to do basic and routine work between meetings, you might discover that they fail to deliver!

- *Their great gift is the capacity for bright ideas,* and they tend to be enthusiastic and to have pet themes. They are often not very practical, and need other people to be prepared to sort out the details, but they will have loads of ideas. Without them committees can be deadly dull!

The realist

- This person prides himself or herself on being down to earth. *They tend to be very good at detail and can make excellent Treasurers or Secretaries!*

- They tend to be good at remembering facts, and can become irritated by the 'never-never' world of the visionaries (who in turn tend to be 'bored' by the contribution of the realists). It is important that committees have both sorts on board. If everyone is an idealist then it is likely that nothing is ever achieved (though some wonderful discussions take place). If everyone is a realist, everything is done perfectly, but routines rule, and few new ideas get explored or carried through.

The soft-hearted

- These are the people who want harmony at all costs! They dislike disagreement and tend to try and avoid any arguments or conflicts on the committee

- They are often 'people centred' and prefer working on things that have a direct relevance to people rather than on more abstract matters. They will often try to avoid tackling any subjects which might make them (or others) feel uncomfortable, and so *there is a danger that hard decisions are not made when they need to be made.* They are usually very friendly, and will go out of their way to get to know you 'as a person'. They may often make a contribution that begins with the words 'I feel that .....'

👍 The tough-minded

- This is the person who likes to get on with the business and is not particularly concerned with chatting about this, that and the other before the meeting. They pride themselves on 'addressing the issues' and like to think that they are single-minded in their approach

- They can often seem to be rather cold and calculating, and they don't seem to mind saying things that could be taken as being a bit harsh or even a bit hurtful to other people on the committee. They are not meaning to be personal - they may be rubbishing an idea that someone has put forward - they are not intending to rubbish the person (but that is not always how it seems, or *feels* if the person being addressed is one of the soft-hearted!). They may often make a contribution that begins with the words 'I think that .....'

👍 The organised one

- This is the person who has all their papers in the right place, they pride themselves on being on time, they probably always sit in the same place and like things to be done in 'the correct way'.

They can sometimes appear to be a bit rigid and predictable, and they are likely to 'play safe' and not take many risks

- This person will almost certainly have thought through the agenda before the meeting, and will not be happy if matters are brought up which have not been notified before the meeting

- They have a tendency to 'think in answers' - that is, they often think that the answer to the problem is quite obvious - just do this, or that, and the problem is solved. They are in danger of reaching conclusions before matters have been thrashed out

- They often appear quite traditional, think that the past ways of approaching issues are the best, and that we should not tamper with something if it is not broken - ie they tend to resist the new and value and conserve tradition.

The provisional one

- This person is in marked contrast to the organised one! They can often appear a bit scatty - their papers are often all mixed up (or probably forgotten or left on the bus), and it is quite likely that they haven't read them before the meeting

- They leave things until the last moment, and so if they were asked to do something at the last meeting, they will only have remembered about it just before the next meeting. They have an ability to jump around an Agenda and so near the end of the meeting they may come up with a bright idea relating to a matter which was discussed an hour earlier - it seems perfectly reasonable to them that the committee should revert to its previous discussion and leave the matter that is under discussion at the moment

• If the organised people value tradition and consistency, then the provisional people value novelty and looseness. If the organisers tend to be hasty to reach a decision, the provisionals tend to be wary of making a decision at all, and even when one is made they are happy for it to be changed straight away! But they are a great asset to a committee when it is going through difficult times of change, because they are able to think themselves into new situations and come up with new ideas.

All mixed up

• Of course, people can be a mixture of different types, and so you can have someone who is an extrovert and also a visionary and also quite provisional, whilst someone may be an introvert, a realist and highly organised.

PREVARICATES
IMPULSIVE
GOOD IN A CRISIS
FLEXIBLE
DREAMS DREAMS

IDEAS PERSON
LIKES NOVELTY
CRITICAL
SEEKS HARMONY
JOYFUL
FLEXIBLE

👍 **What these categories do is give us some general idea which can help us to understand why people react in the ways that they do.**

**Opposites sometimes
don't mix very well**

- If people are very different from each other, they may find that they get irritated by each other. But remember, the person who drives you round the bend by their attitudes may be experiencing just the same sorts of feelings about you!

- Ideally, of course, we learn to value contributions that other people can make; and ideally they value the contribution that we can make

- It all helps to make committees more interesting

- Remember - if the subject of the committee meeting is deadly - you can always gain something from it by observing the way that people operate!

*Handy tip: If you are interested in learning more about different personality types, see **Knowing Me, Knowing You** by Malcolm Goldsmith and Martin Wharton, published by SPCK, 1993.*

18   A Committee is only a Committee

Do not lose sleep over what happens at a committee meeting - it is only a committee, it is not life!

Committees are a very useful way of getting things done.

They can also be a way of ensuring that nothing gets done - check out what your committee is trying to do (or not do).

Remember that all the usual insights that apply to groups are also relevant to committees, because a committee is just one particular sort of group. People can play many different types of games when they operate in groups, some of them conscious but many of them are unconscious.

Handy tip: Make sure that you are as aware as possible of the games that some people on your committee might be playing. *Michael and Maggie Kindred have explored these issues in the companion booklet to this one:* **Once upon a group** *(£5.00, plus £1.00 post and packing, from 4M Publications)*

- Preparation is all-important. If you work at the material to be discussed before you go to the meeting, it is likely that you will be able to make a contribution, and also that you will feel at ease. You might be one of the lucky people who can turn up without preparation and make the most amazing and world-changing observations - but then again, you might not have acquired those skills yet. So prepare!

- And don't be bullied! You have every right to be there and your voice is as important as anyone else's - so speak up, don't shut up! But also recognise that someone else might have a better approach than yours, so be prepared to listen and to support those ideas which seem sensible.

- **Remember what the purpose of the committee is - and enjoy your time on it.**

Index

Accounts
  annual 24, 26, 27
  audited 24, 27
Accounts, bank - see Bank accounts
Accurate records - see Records
Action column 48, 49
Agenda 19, 22, 28-33
Annual General Meeting (AGM) 24
Any Other Business (AOB) 31, 33, 42-46
Any Other Concerned Business (AOCB) 31
Apologies 29, 33, 42, 44, 46, 48, 60
Attendance 59, 60
  record 60
Bank accounts 24, 26
  mandate form 26
Budgets 15, 27
Casting vote 38
Chairperson (Chair, Chairman, Chairwoman, Convenor) 13, 14, 18-20
  Rotating 14
  Vice Chairperson 14
Cheque authorisation 26
Committee
  boundaries 6
  comfort of members 7
  Executive 53, 54
  focus 8
  Golden Rules 5
  joining 9-12
  Management 4
  objectives 5, 19
  past history 10, 11
  pendant 56
  process 6
  purpose 5, 8
  responsibilities 5, 6
  shape 6
  structure 6
  Standing 53, 54
  style 12, 17
  Sub- committee 55, 56
    Finance 56
  terms of reference 8, 19
Communication styles 6
Confidentiality 7, 17, 36, 50, 51, 52
Confidential Minutes and Book 50, 51
Consensus 36
Constitution 11, 24, 36, 57, 58, 59
Convenor - see Chairperson
Co-opted Members 16
Correspondence 22, 23, 29, 33
Date of next meeting - see Meeting, date of next
Decisions, decision-making 4, 5, 22, 36, 37, 40, 59
Disagreements 36, 37, 38
Election, standing for 24
Employment of staff 27
Executive Committee - see Committee
Expense Claims Forms 15, 23, 26
Expenses, payment 26
Files 24
Finance 25, 42, 44, 46, 48
Financial advice 27
Float 27
'In attendance' 17
Inquorate meetings 59
Invoices, payment 26
Length of meeting 31, 32
Length of service 11, 13, 14, 16, 57
Majority, simple and two-thirds 36
Management committee - see Committee
Matters arising 30, 33, 42, 44, 46, 48

Meeting, date of next 48, 49
Membership 57
Minutes 40-49
   draft copy 23
   numbering of items 41
Minutes Secretary - see Secretary
Model agenda 32, 33
Motions 36
Nem con 37
Number of meetings 58
Observers 17, 51
Officer/Office Holders 16, 57
Ordinary members 16
Parent body 15, 51, 55, 56
Pendant committees - see Committee
Preparation 5, 70
Press 51, 52
Process - see Committee
Proposer 35
Proposals 35, 36
Proposing a motion 34-38
Quorum 58, 59
Receipts 26, 27
Records, accurate 7, 24, 26, 40
Refreshments 7, 22
Resignations 39
Resolutions 35, 36
Rotating Chairperson - see Chairperson
Seconder 35
Secretary 15, 21-24
   Minutes Secretary 15, 24
Secret vote - see Vote, secret
Standing Committee - see Committee
Standing Orders 58, 59
Structure - see Committee
Sub-committee - see Committee
Telephone calls 24, 27
Terms of reference - see Committee
Timekeeping 7, 20
Travelling expenses 27
Treasurer 15, 25-27
Treasurer's Report 29, 33

Value judgement 43
Vice Chairperson - see Chairperson
Vote, secret 36
Voting 15, 16, 17, 24, 35-38